My Creative Diary

An Inspiring and Empowering Book for Girls with Activities to Boost Creativity, Confidence and Self-Esteem

Sav Lucia

My Creative Diary

An Inspiring and Empowering Book for Girls with Activities to Boost Creativity, Confidence and Self-Esteem

Published by Special Art Books
www.specialartbooks.com

Paperback ISBN: 9791255532149

Cover Art by Karmina Art
Images © Shutterstock and Envato

This diary belongs to:

My age:

My favorite color:

My favorite thing to do is:

TABLE OF CONTENTS

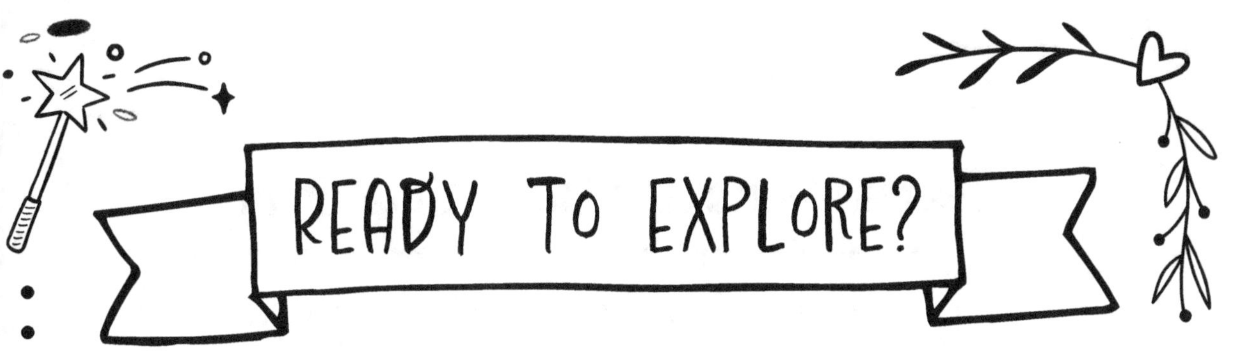

Welcome to this special place for you to explore your creative self. Whenever you open these pages it's a chance to connect to your thoughts, dreams, and ideas without judgment. Here you are invited to express yourself without worry and to explore who you are becoming as you grow up.

Let your imagination run wild, and know that there is no such thing as a bad idea. Don't ever doubt how unique and intelligent you are, and the potential that you hold. And remember that there is so much of you waiting to be discovered.

As you dive into these pages, let yourself be open. Be proud of your perspective and embrace your creative mind. One day you'll be able to look back at these pages and see how much you've grown, but for now enjoy the moment.

You are amazing just the way you are.
Now let's explore all there is to you.

Testing Pens and Color Swatching

Test your pens here! Draw a rainbow with your favorite colors.

Circle the words that best describe who you are.

Confident
Creative
Adventurous
Energetic
Outgoing
Optimistic
Resilient
Curious
Intelligent
Resourceful
Kind-hearted

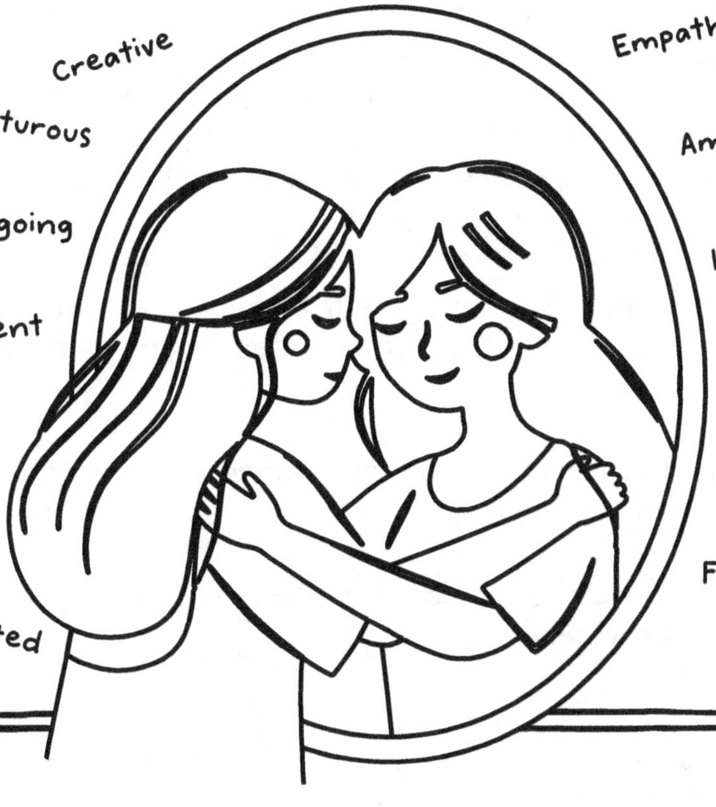

Empathetic
Compassionate
Ambitious
Thoughtful
Imaginative
Playful
Caring
Determined
Brave
Unique
Friendly
Expressive

"One child . . . one book,
one pen can change the world."

-Malala Yousafzai

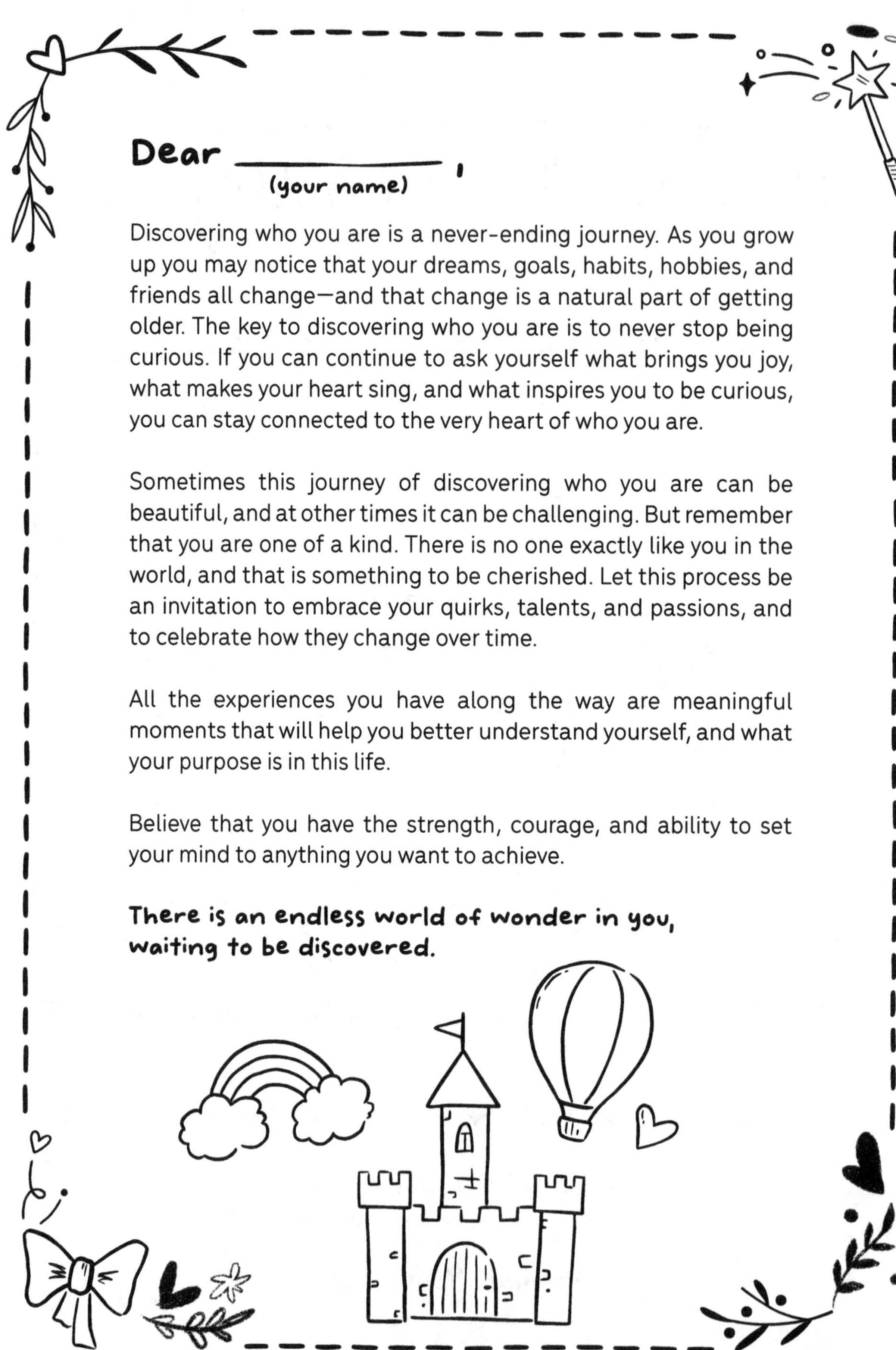

Dear ___________,
(your name)

Discovering who you are is a never-ending journey. As you grow up you may notice that your dreams, goals, habits, hobbies, and friends all change—and that change is a natural part of getting older. The key to discovering who you are is to never stop being curious. If you can continue to ask yourself what brings you joy, what makes your heart sing, and what inspires you to be curious, you can stay connected to the very heart of who you are.

Sometimes this journey of discovering who you are can be beautiful, and at other times it can be challenging. But remember that you are one of a kind. There is no one exactly like you in the world, and that is something to be cherished. Let this process be an invitation to embrace your quirks, talents, and passions, and to celebrate how they change over time.

All the experiences you have along the way are meaningful moments that will help you better understand yourself, and what your purpose is in this life.

Believe that you have the strength, courage, and ability to set your mind to anything you want to achieve.

There is an endless world of wonder in you, waiting to be discovered.

In this section, you will have an opportunity to discover yourself.
We will explore self-identity, confidence, individuality, strengths,
dreams, talents, values, and ask ourselves what it means to grow.

SELF-IDENTITY:
"I am proud of who
I am becoming."

CONFIDENCE:
"I believe in myself
and my abilities."

INDIVIDUALITY:
"I celebrate what makes
me unique and special."

STRENGTHS:
"I recognize and
appreciate my strengths."

DREAMS:
"I have the power to imagine
and achieve my dreams."

TALENTS:
"I am discovering new
talents every day."

VALUES:
"I understand and
honor what is
important to me."

GROWTH:
"I embrace change and
am always learning
and growing."

My Artistic Selfie!
Draw yourself one year ago.
Draw who you think you'll be one year from now.
Draw yourself as you feel today.

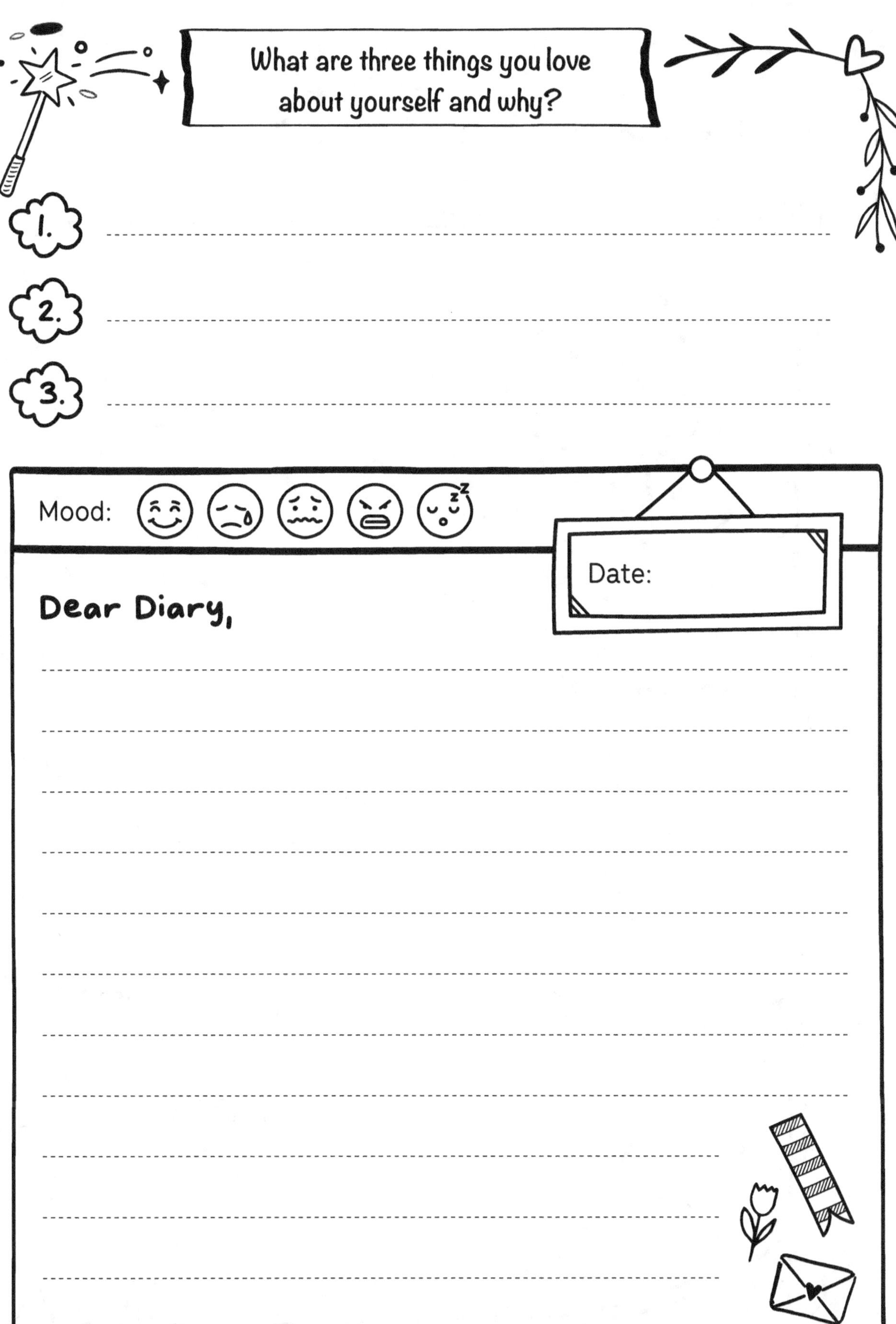

What are three things you love about yourself and why?
1.
2.
3.
Mood:
Date:
Dear Diary,

My Dream Map

What are your dreams? What do you want to achieve?
Where do you want to go? Use magazine cut-outs, drawings, and words to make a vision.
N
W
E
S

What are your favorite things?
Why do you love them?
My Favorites
Movie
TV Show
Book
Food

What are your biggest strengths?

How do they help you in your daily life? How can you use your strength to help others around you?

Mood:

Date:

Dear Diary,

We all have
different gifts.

Zesty
Purifying
Aromatic
Resilient
Vibrant
Soothing
Versatile
Calming
Romantic
Refreshing

What Makes Me Special

Mood:

Date:

Dear Diary,

My Wonderful Life

Draw or write important moments from your past.

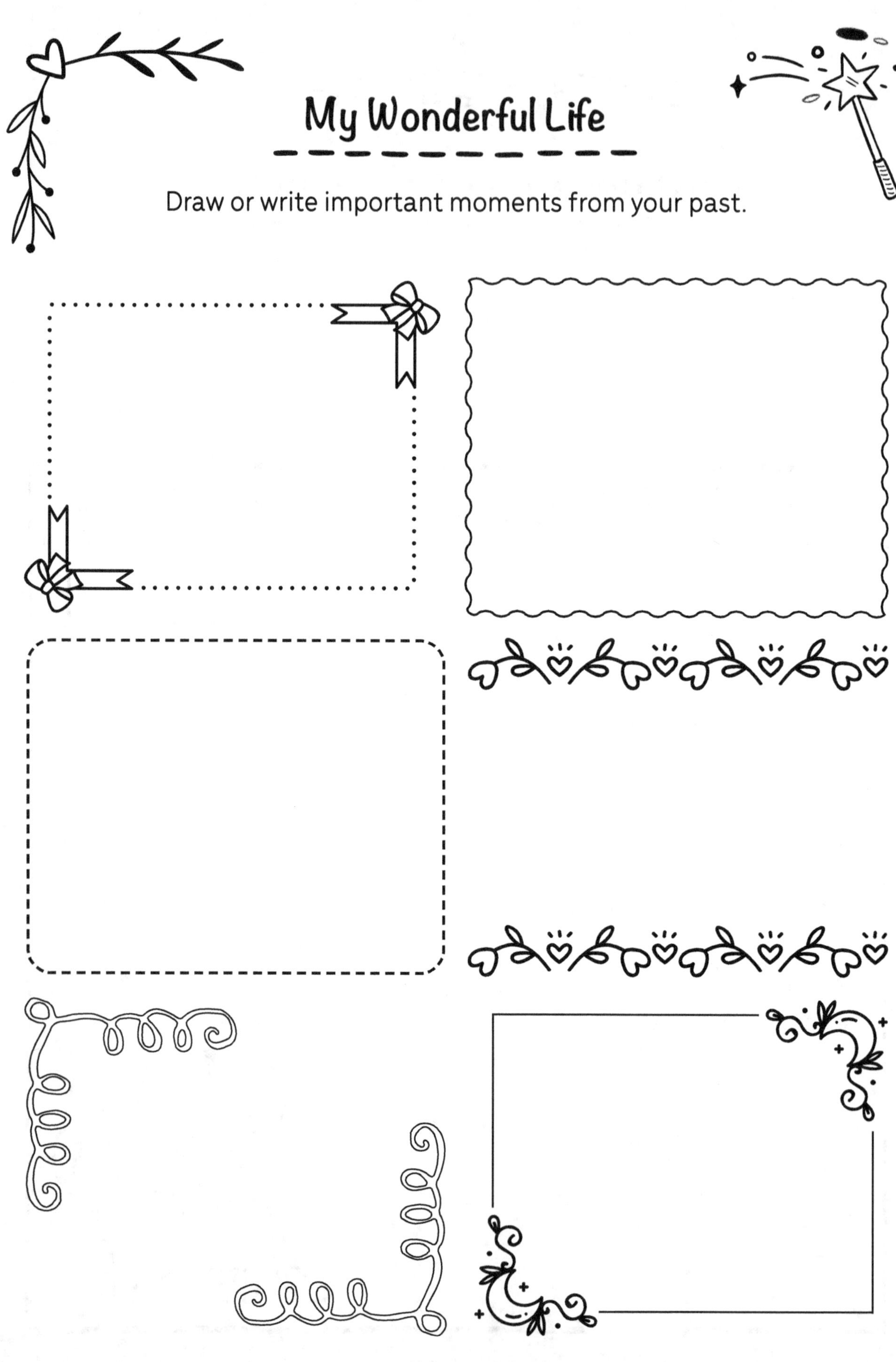

What did you learn from these experiences that you will remember?

Drawing My Own Paper Doll

Using the outline provided, draw a doll and design her wardrobe.
Use separate sheets or cardboard to cut them out and play.

What are some challenges you've faced
and how did you overcome them?

Mood:

Date:

Dear Diary,

My Perfect Day
Morning
Breakfast
Activity 1
Lunch

Activity 2
Evening
Dinner
Bedtime

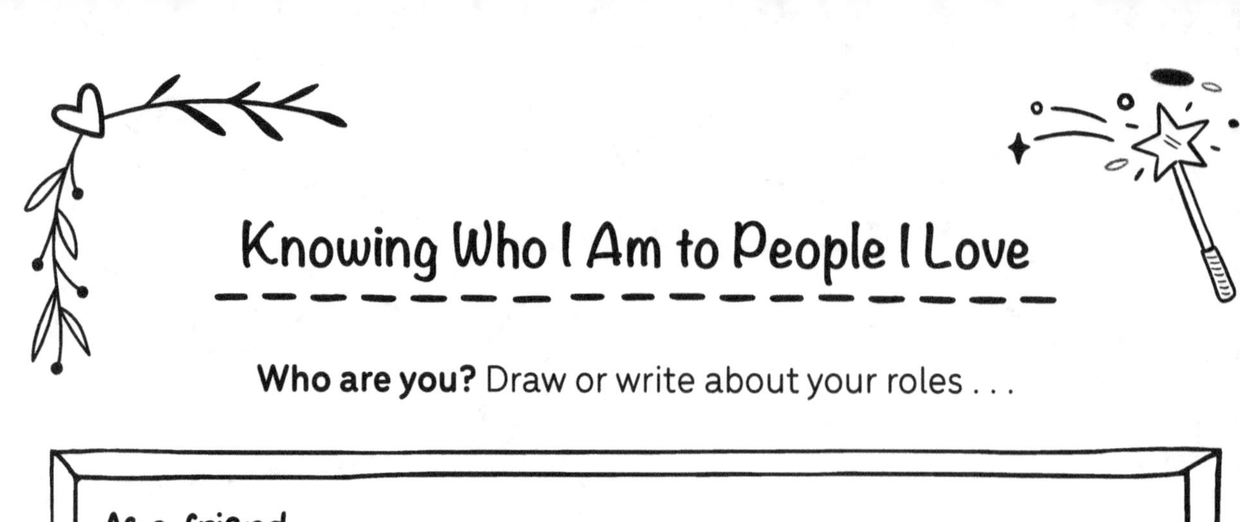

Knowing Who I Am to People I Love

Who are you? Draw or write about your roles . . .

As a friend

As a daughter

As a sister

As a granddaughter

As a student

Mood:

Date:

Dear Diary,

What are three goals you want to achieve in the next year?

How will you work towards them?

Why are these goals important to you?

BOUNDLESS CREATIVITY
"What you do makes a difference, and you have to decide what kind of difference you want to make."
-Jane Goodall

Dear ______________,
(your name)

Each one of us has a creative voice inside. The challenge is often learning how to understand and listen to that voice, communicate, and channel it into something. For some people it may be dancing, for others singing, art, or acting. There are so many ways you can use this creative voice to solve problems, express emotions, convey ideas, and build things that can make the world a better place.

Every time you create something, you bring part of yourself into the world. Maybe that is your unique perspective, emotions, or dreams. Whichever way you choose to express your creative voice, let yourself be heard.

This creative voice keeps you connected to the heart of who you are and can encourage you to experiment, be curious, laugh, and have fun in the process. Embrace your imagination, and let go of perfection. The creation process is one that is meant for expression and learning, no matter how big or small.

Remember that your ideas can inspire others, bring joy to yourself and those around you, and make a difference in shaping the world around you.

Let your creative light shine. After all there is boundless creativity inside you waiting to be unleashed.

In this section, you will unleash your boundless creativity. We will dive into imagination, innovation, artistry, exploration, inspiration, expression, originality, and freedom to create without limits.

IMAGINATION:

"I let my imagination run free and explore new ideas."

INNOVATION:

"I am a creator of new and exciting ideas."

ARTISTRY:

"I express myself through my unique artistic abilities."

EXPLORATION:

"I love trying new things and exploring new possibilities."

INSPIRATION:

"I find inspiration in everything around me."

EXPRESSION:

"I share my unique voice and creativity with confidence."

ORIGINALITY:

"I am one of a kind and my creations are original."

FREEDOM:

"I create without limits and embrace my creative freedom."

Go outside and find items like leaves, flowers, and rocks. Use these to create your own nature art. Glue them here or draw a picture of what you made.

Describe a place in nature that makes you feel happy and peaceful. Why do you love it?

Mood:

Date:

Dear Diary,

My Magical World

What does your fantasy world look like? Create a large-scale map of an imaginary world. Draw mountains, castles, rivers, forests, magical creatures, hidden treasures, and any magical element you'd love to see in your world!

My Art Gallery

Fill this gallery with your favorite pieces of art. It can be your own drawings, photos of things you've made, or any piece of art that inspires you.

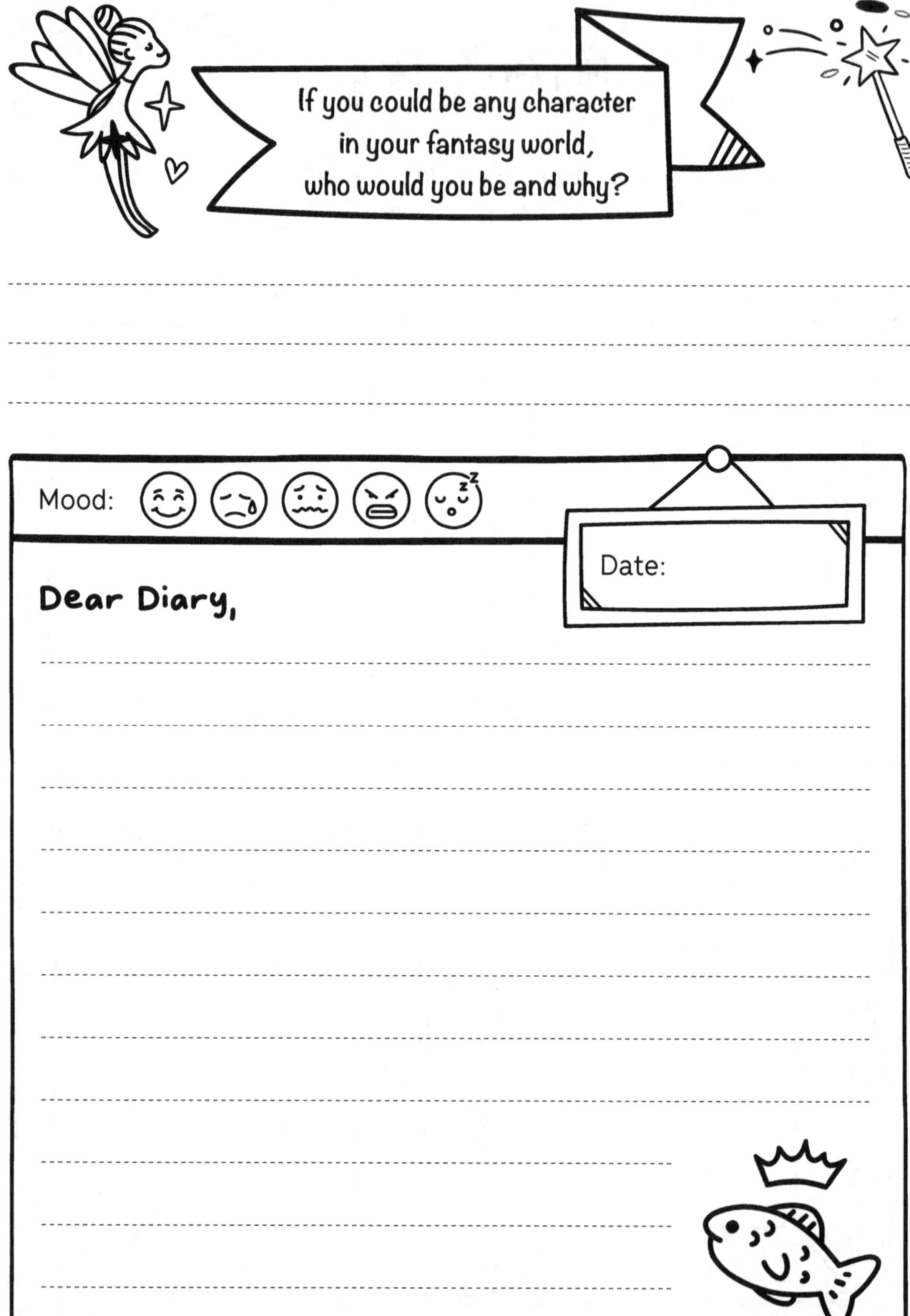

Mood:

Date:

Dear Diary,

"Art is an opportunity to
bring your soul into form."

-Deeyah Khan

My Dream Outfit

Design your dream outfit. What colors, patterns, and styles do you love?

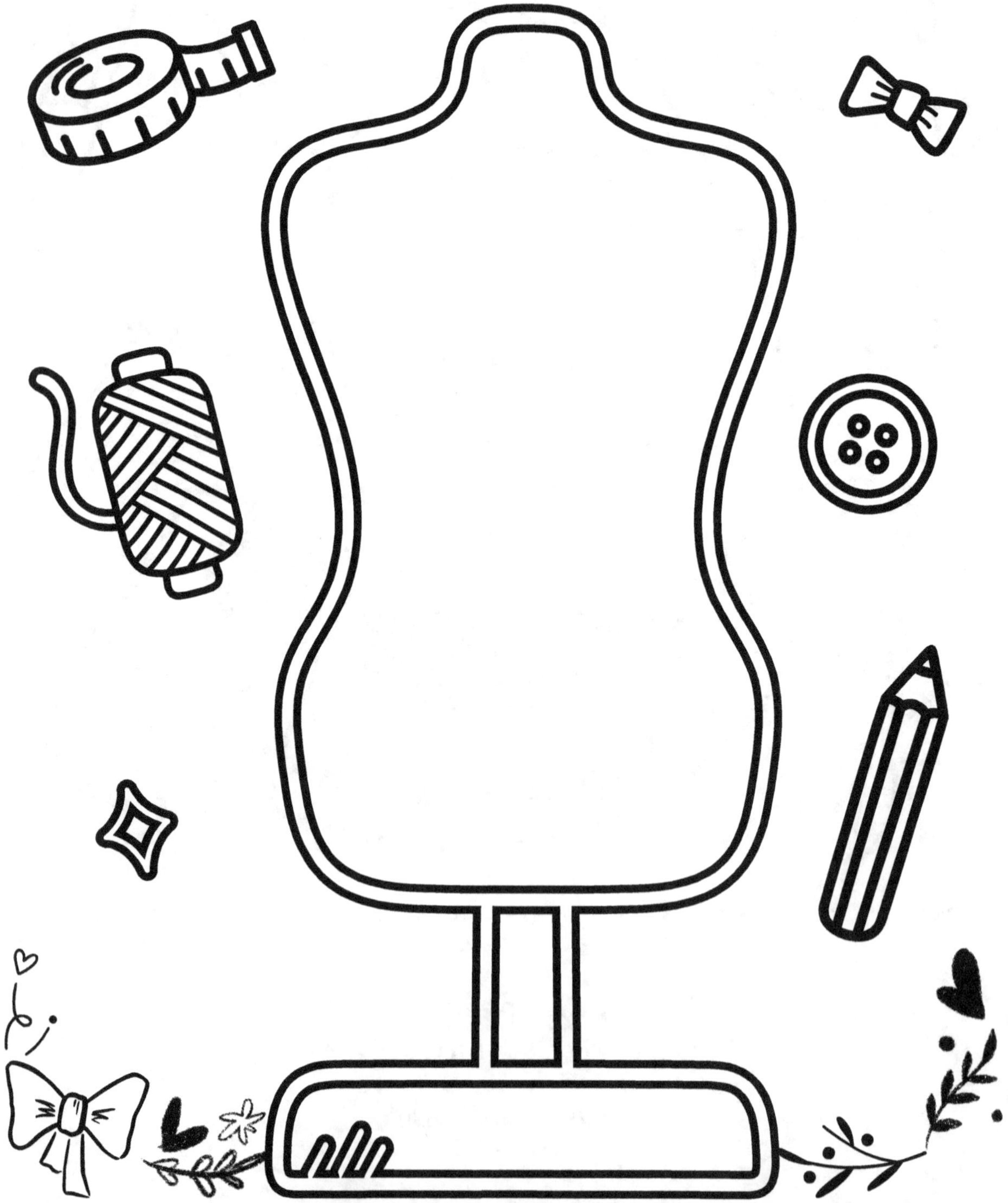

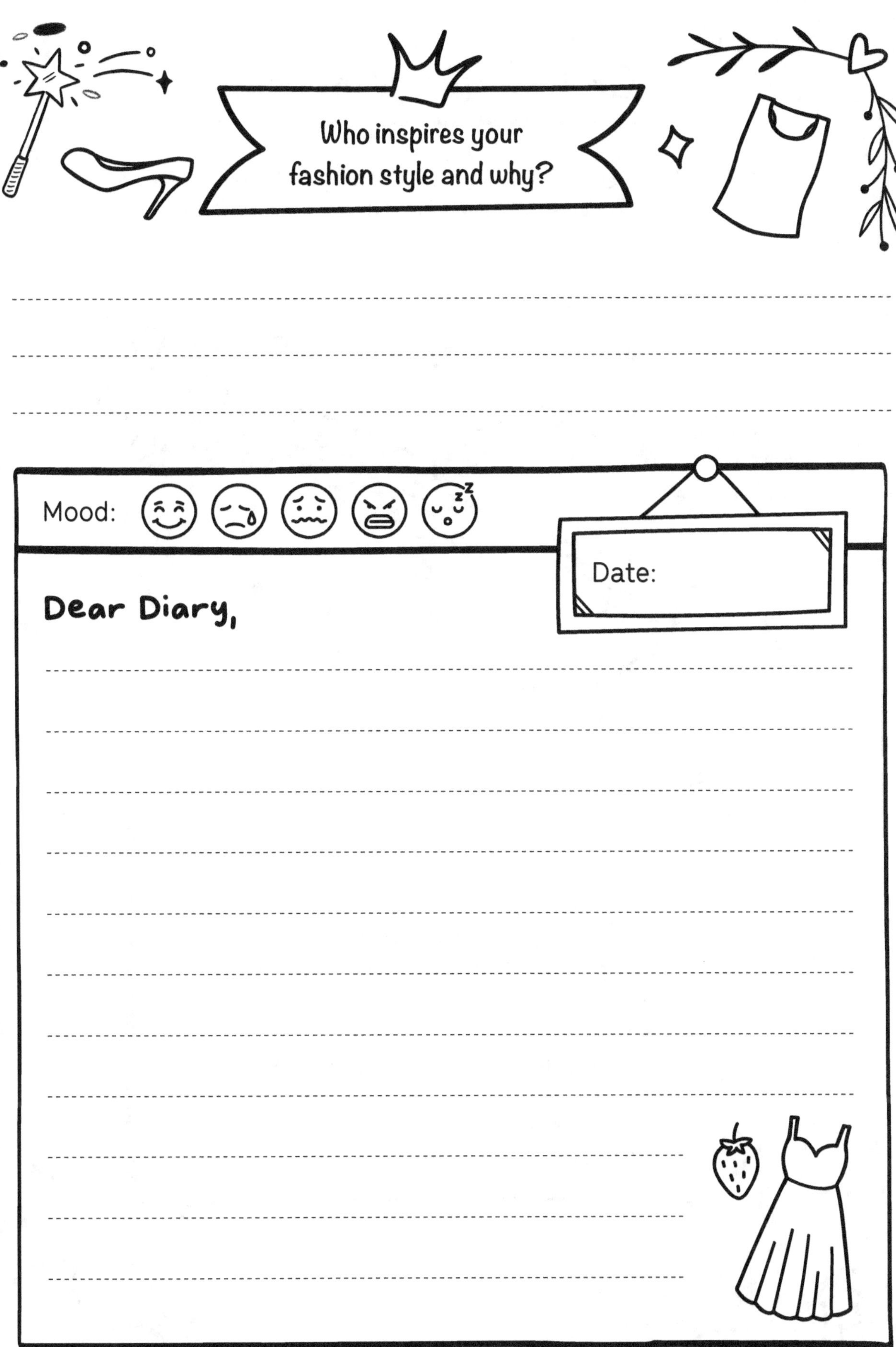

Who inspires your
fashion style and why?

Mood:

Date:

Dear Diary,

Craft Corner: Mini Banjo

Create your own mini paper banjo and then put on
a musical performance for your friends and family.

MATERIALS NEEDED:

- Paper plates (2)
- Cardboard tube (from a paper towel roll)
- String or yarn (4 pieces, about 12 inches each)
- Glue or tape
- Scissors
- Markers, crayons, or paint (for decorating)
- A small piece of cardboard or sturdy paper
  (for the bridge)
- Hole punch (optional)

INSTRUCTIONS:

1. Prepare the Banjo Body:
    • Take one paper plate and cut out the center, leaving a ring about 2 inches wide. This will be the front of the banjo.
    • If desired, you can punch four holes evenly spaced around the edge of the plate ring. This is where the strings will be threaded.

2. Decorate the Banjo:
    • Decorate both paper plates using markers, crayons, or paint. Encourage creativity with colors, patterns, and designs. Let the plates dry if you used paint.

3. Attach the Plates:
    • Place the intact paper plate face down. This will be the back of the banjo.
    • Glue or tape the decorated ring (the front) onto the back plate. Make sure to leave a space at the bottom where the cardboard tube will be attached.

4. Prepare the Neck:
    • Take the cardboard tube and cut a slit on one end about 2 inches deep. This will help secure the tube to the plates.
    • Decorate the tube with markers or paint.

5. Attach the Neck:
    • Insert the cut end of the tube into the space between the two plates. Secure it with glue or tape.

6. Add the Strings:
    • If you punched holes in the plate, thread the strings through the holes and tie them securely.
    • Alternatively, if you didn't punch holes, tape or glue one end of each string to the back of the intact plate, stretching them across the center hole and securing the other end to the opposite side of the plate.

7. Create the Bridge:
    • Cut a small piece of cardboard or sturdy paper (about 2 inches long and 1 inch wide). Fold it in half lengthwise to create a "V" shape.
    • Place the "V" shape under the strings near the center of the banjo to act as a bridge, lifting the strings slightly above the plate.

8. Final Touches:
    • Ensure all parts are securely attached.
    • Let any glue dry completely.

OPTIONAL:

• You can add tuning pegs by gluing small buttons or beads to the top of the cardboard tube.
• Create a strap using a piece of string or ribbon and attach it to the neck and body for a more realistic look.

Seasonal Scenes

What's your favorite thing to do in each season?
Draw a scene for spring, summer, fall, and winter.

Spring

Summer

Autumn

Winter

What's your favorite season and why?
What special memories do you have from that season?

Mood:

Date:

Dear Diary,

The Artist's Maze

Help the artist find their way through the maze to their canvas!

You are your
own masterpiece!

Writing My Own Poem

Write a poem about someone or something you love. Here's how:

INSTRUCTIONS:

1. Choose a Subject: Think about someone or something you love. It could be a person, a pet, a place, or even an object that makes you happy.

2. Describe with Senses: Use your senses to describe your subject. How does it look, sound, feel, smell, or taste? For example, if you're writing about your pet dog, describe its fur, its bark, the way it makes you feel when it cuddles with you.

3. Think about Emotions: What emotions does your subject make you feel? Joy, love, excitement? Try to convey these emotions in your poem.

4. Use Similes and Metaphors: These are comparisons that can make your poem more vivid. A simile uses "like" or "as" (e.g., "Her smile is like sunshine"), while a metaphor states something is something else (e.g., "He is a shining star").

5. Structure Your Poem: Poems can have any structure, but you might start with a few lines or what are called stanzas. Each stanza can focus on a different aspect of your subject.

6. Be Yourself: There are no rules in poetry. Use your unique voice and style to express yourself.

(poem title)

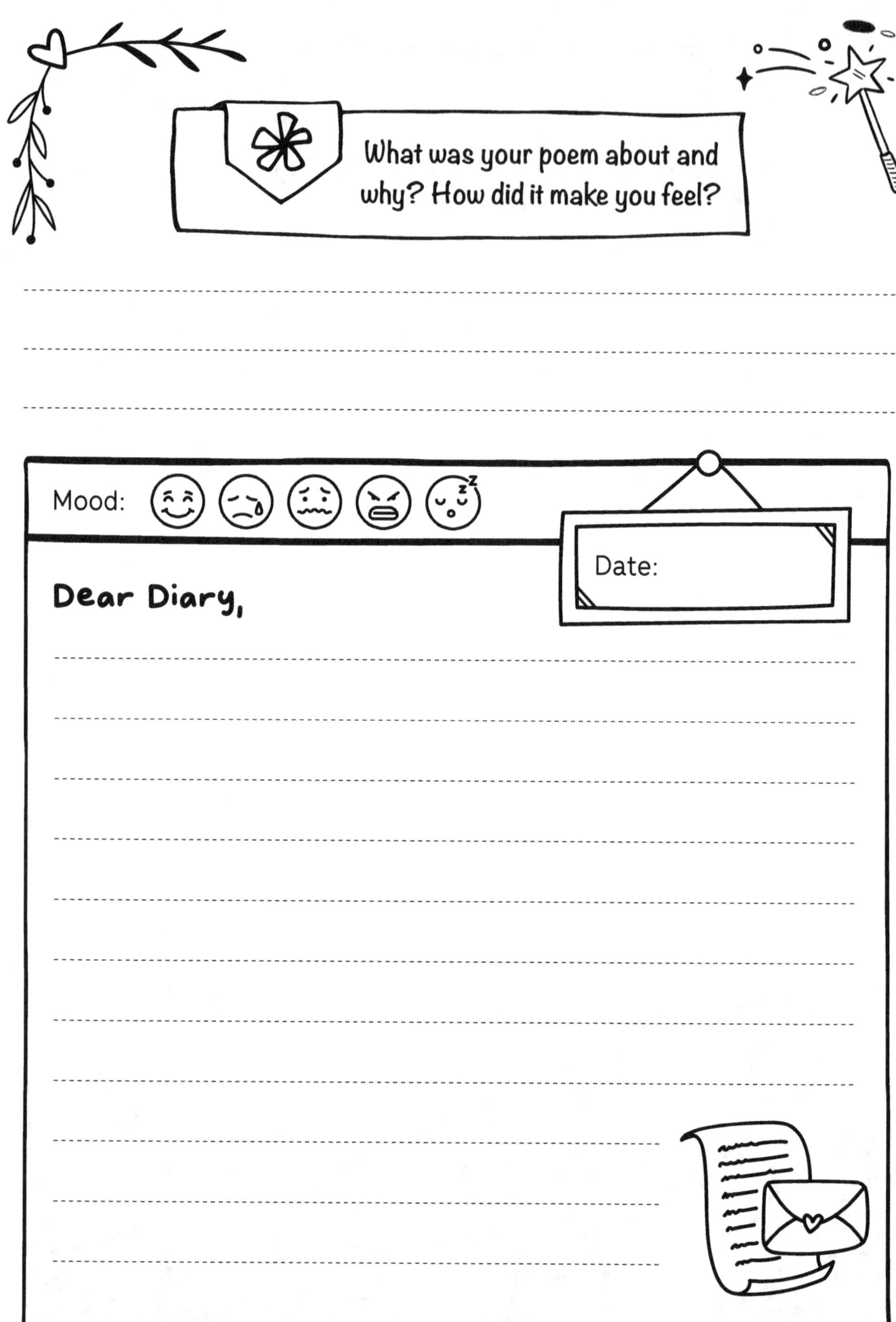

What was your poem about and why? How did it make you feel?

Mood:

Date:

Dear Diary,

EXPRESS YOUR FEELINGS
"You may not control all the events that happen to you, but you can decide not to be reduced by them."
-Maya Angelou

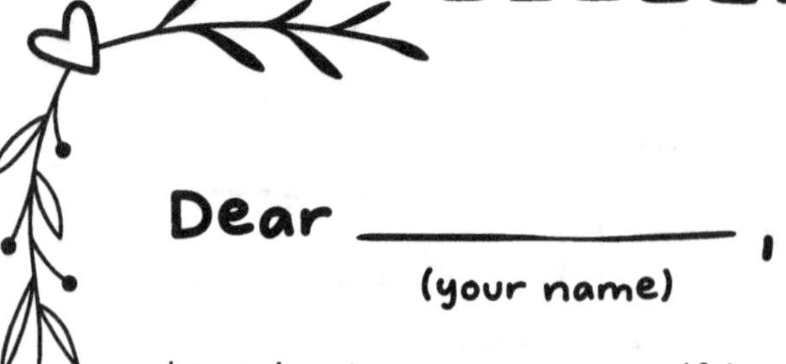

Learning to express yourself is an essential part of growing up, but before we can communicate our needs to others, we often need to find time and space to be with ourselves. This journal is an opportunity to slow down and be with yourself. When you take time to sit down and draw, write, or color here you might ask yourself: How do I feel today? How does the way I feel change the way I am with my friends or family?

You might think of your emotions like colors—each color represents a different way to feel. Some colors you may like more than others, but at the same time there is beauty in seeing all the colors come together like a rainbow.

Your feelings may change a lot too, and that's okay. Most of the time our feelings are just passing by like the wind. They come, they go, and they change moment to moment. The secret to life is to let yourself feel everything: be happy, joyful, sad, scared, angry . . . Your feelings are there to tell you something you need to know. Usually they have some wisdom to offer you about how a person, place, or activity makes you feel. Listen to that wisdom when you hear your heart offering it to you.

Let your heart be open to whatever it feels, and remember that when you step into your feelings you can find freedom in being your authentic self.

In this section, you will learn to express your feelings. We will explore emotions, communication, honesty, vulnerability, support, connection, reflection, and courage to face your emotions bravely.

EMOTIONS:
"I understand and
embrace all
of my emotions."

COMMUNICATION:
"I share my thoughts
and feelings openly
and honestly."

HONESTY:
"I am true
to myself and
my feelings."

VULNERABILITY:
"I allow myself
to be open
and vulnerable."

SUPPORT:
"I seek and
give support
when needed."

CONNECTION:
"I build deep
and meaningful
relationships."

REFLECTION:
"I take time to reflect
on my feelings
and experiences."

COURAGE:
"I face my emotions
with courage
and strength."

Mood Tracker

Take a moment each day to sit down and notice how you feel. How do your feelings affect your day and everyone around you? Can you notice any patterns between how you feel and your responsibilities on different days?

Color each petal with your mood for the day.

Orange – Happy

Yellow – Content

Blue – Tired

Green – Sad

Mood:

Date:

Dear Diary,

Express with Colors

Color the illustrations below. Use colors that match how you feel when you're experiencing the different emotions in each illustration.

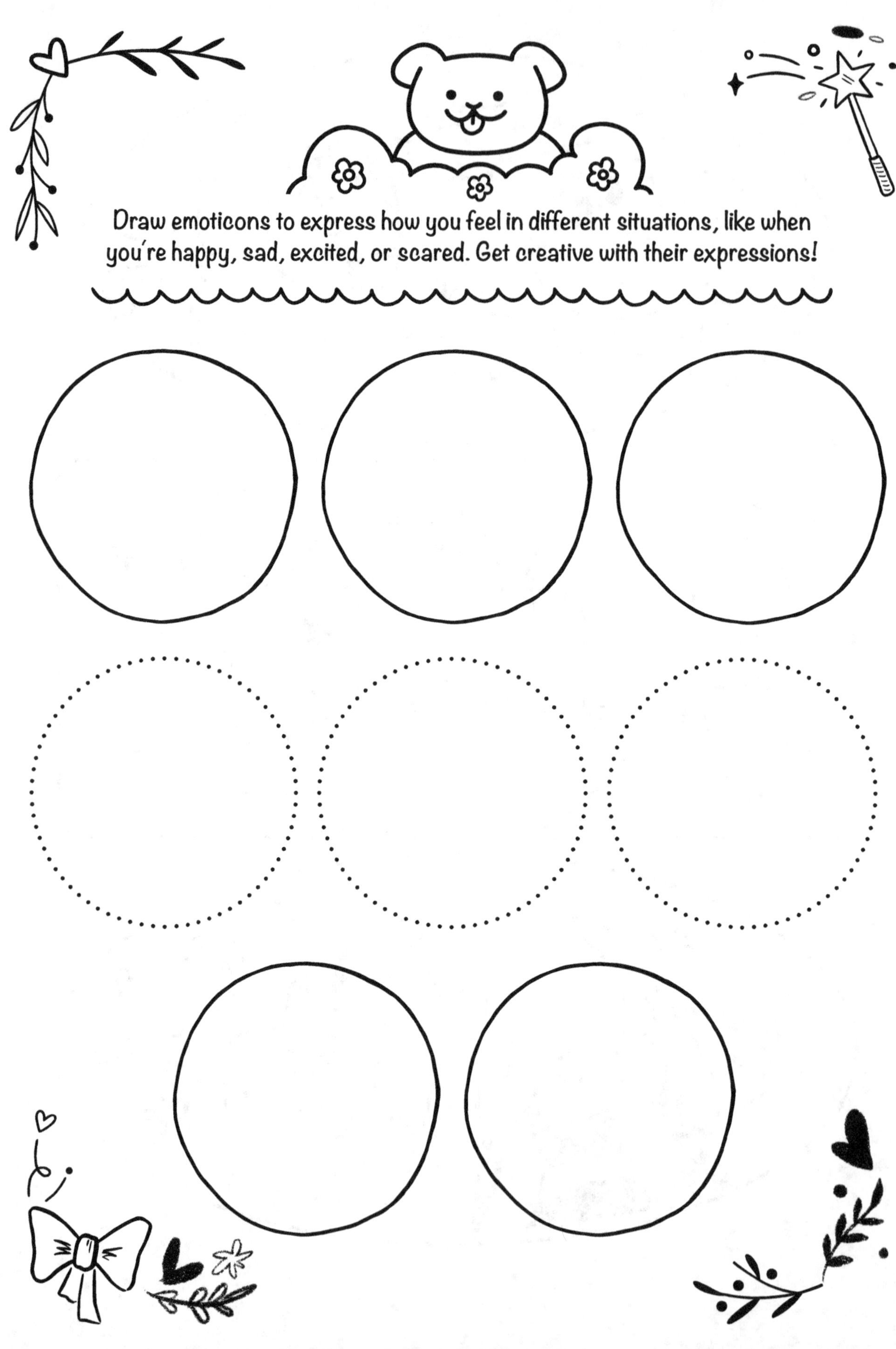

Draw emoticons to express how you feel in different situations, like when you're happy, sad, excited, or scared. Get creative with their expressions!

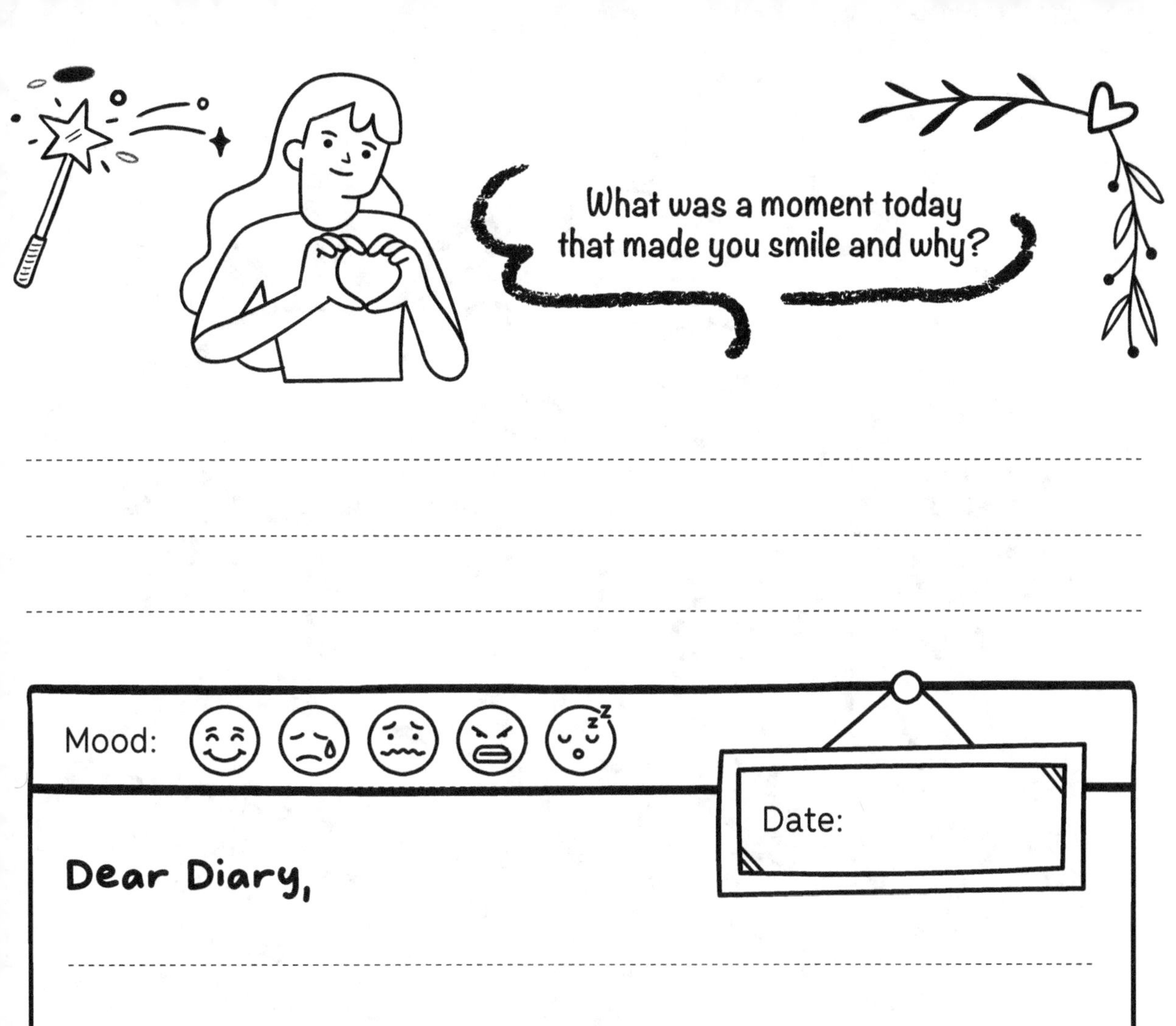

Mood:

Date:

Dear Diary,

"A champion is defined not by their wins but by how they recover when they fall."
-Serena Williams

Feelings Wheel

Use the feelings wheel to find the perfect words for your emotions.
Write about a time you felt a mix of different feelings.

Sad

Fear

Calm

Anger

Happy

Strong

Rejected, Hopeless, Betrayed, Helpless, Unmotivated, Disappointed, Peaceful, Relaxed, Sentimental, Contented, Optimistic, Accepting, Satisfied, Amused, Enthusiastic, Pleased, Excited, Passionate

Isolated, Ashamed, Neglected, Lonely, Weak, Hurt, Relieved, Mellow, Trusting, Focused, Present, Comfortable, Jolly, Delighted, Blissful, Joyful, Fun, Cheerful

Anxious, Skeptical, Overwhelmed, Tense, Paranoid, Confused, Insecure, Nervous, Panicky, Worried, Shocked, Stressed

Fearless, Worthy, Valued, Respected, Powerful, Proud, Confident, Intelligent, Successful, Empowered, Determined, Important

Rage, Annoyed, Bitter, Hateful, Grumpy, Jealous, Frustrated, Aggravated, Disgusted, Aggressive, Hostile, Irritated

Write about a time when you felt proud of yourself. What did you do? How did it make you feel?

Mood:

Date:

Dear Diary,

FEEL in the Blanks

Word bank for emotions:

HAPPY: Feeling really good and smiling a lot.

SAD: Feeling down and maybe wanting to cry.

ANGRY: Feeling mad and upset, like when something isn't fair.

EXCITED: Feeling super happy and looking forward to something.

SCARED: Feeling afraid, like when something seems dangerous or spooky.

SURPRISED: Feeling suddenly amazed or shocked by something unexpected.

NERVOUS: Feeling a little scared and worried about something coming up.

CONTENT: Feeling calm and satisfied, like everything is just right.

CONFUSED: Feeling mixed up and not sure what is happening.

DISAPPOINTED: Feeling sad because something didn't go as hoped.

PROUD: Feeling really good about something you did well.

HOPEFUL: Feeling good about the future and expecting good things.

GRATEFUL: Feeling thankful and happy for something nice.

JEALOUS: Feeling upset because you want what someone else has.

LONELY: Feeling sad because you want to be with others but aren't.

EMBARRASSED: Feeling uncomfortable because you
did something silly or wrong.

GUILTY: Feeling bad because you did something wrong or hurt someone.

FRUSTRATED: Feeling annoyed because something is hard to do.

BORED: Feeling tired and uninterested because nothing fun is happening.

ANXIOUS: Feeling very worried and nervous about something.

CURIOUS: Feeling eager to learn or know more about something.

CALM: Feeling relaxed and not worried or upset.

JOYFUL: Feeling very happy and full of joy.

ASHAMED: Feeling bad about something
wrong you did and wanting to hide.

RELIEVED: Feeling happy and relaxed because something bad is over.

INSPIRED: Feeling excited to do something creative or good.

DETERMINED: Feeling strong about trying hard to do something.

OVERWHELMED: Feeling like there's too much to handle all at once.

PLAYFUL: Feeling happy and wanting to play and have fun.

AFFECTIONATE: Feeling loving and wanting to show you care about someone.

SHOCKED: Feeling very surprised in a big way.

PEACEFUL: Feeling very calm and without any worries.

SYMPATHETIC: Feeling sorry for someone who is having a hard time.

EMPATHETIC: Feeling like you understand and share another person's feelings.

ANNOYED: Feeling a little angry because something is bothering you.

REJECTED: Feeling sad because someone didn't accept or include you.

MISCHIEVOUS: Feeling like doing something a little naughty but fun.

TRIUMPHANT: Feeling very happy because you achieved something great.

SATISFIED: Feeling happy because something turned out well.

WORRIED: Feeling uneasy and thinking something bad might happen.

EAGER: Feeling very excited and ready to do something.

INDIFFERENT: Feeling like you don't care much about something.

AMUSED: Feeling entertained and finding something funny.

SERENE: Feeling very calm and peaceful.

DISTRUSTFUL: Feeling like you can't trust someone or something.

OPTIMISTIC: Feeling hopeful and thinking good things will happen.

SKEPTICAL: Feeling doubtful and not sure if something is true or right.

INSECURE: Feeling unsure about yourself and lacking confidence.

SECURE: Feeling safe, confident, and sure about yourself.

When my parents hug me, I feel ______________.

When my friend shares their snack with me, I feel ______________.

When I get a good grade on a test, I feel ______________.

When I forget my homework, I feel ______________.

When I play with my pet, I feel ______________.

When my favorite team wins a game, I feel ______________.

When I hear my favorite song, I feel ______________.

When I wake up early for a special trip, I feel ______________.

When someone compliments me, I feel ______________.

When I have to speak in front of the class, I feel ______________.

When I try something new, I feel ______________.

When I have a bad dream, I feel ______________.

When I help someone in need, I feel ______________.

When I argue with a friend, I feel ______________.

When it's my birthday, I feel ______________.

When it's raining outside and I can't play, I feel ______________.

When I finish a big project, I feel ______________.

When I get in trouble, I feel ______________.

When I spend time with my family, I feel ______________.

When I am alone, I feel ______________.

When I see a beautiful sunset, I feel ______________.

When I lose something important, I feel ______________.

Writing My Own Song

Write your own song or the lyrics of a favorite song that makes you feel good. Why does this song make you feel this way?

What song always makes you dance and why?
Describe how it feels to dance to this song.

Mood:

Date:

Dear Diary,

My Emotions
Collage
Happiness
Sadness
Anger
Surprise

Find and paste a photo or magazine cutout that shows happiness, sadness, anger, surprise, and forgiveness.
Explain why these images represent those emotions to you.

Forgiveness

Things That Make Me Feel

List things that make you feel happy, sad, annoyed, and angry.
Why do they make you feel this way?

Happy

- ♡ ....
- ♡ ....
- ♡ ....
- ♡ ....

Sad

- ♡ ....
- ♡ ....
- ♡ ....
- ♡ ....

Annoyed

Angry

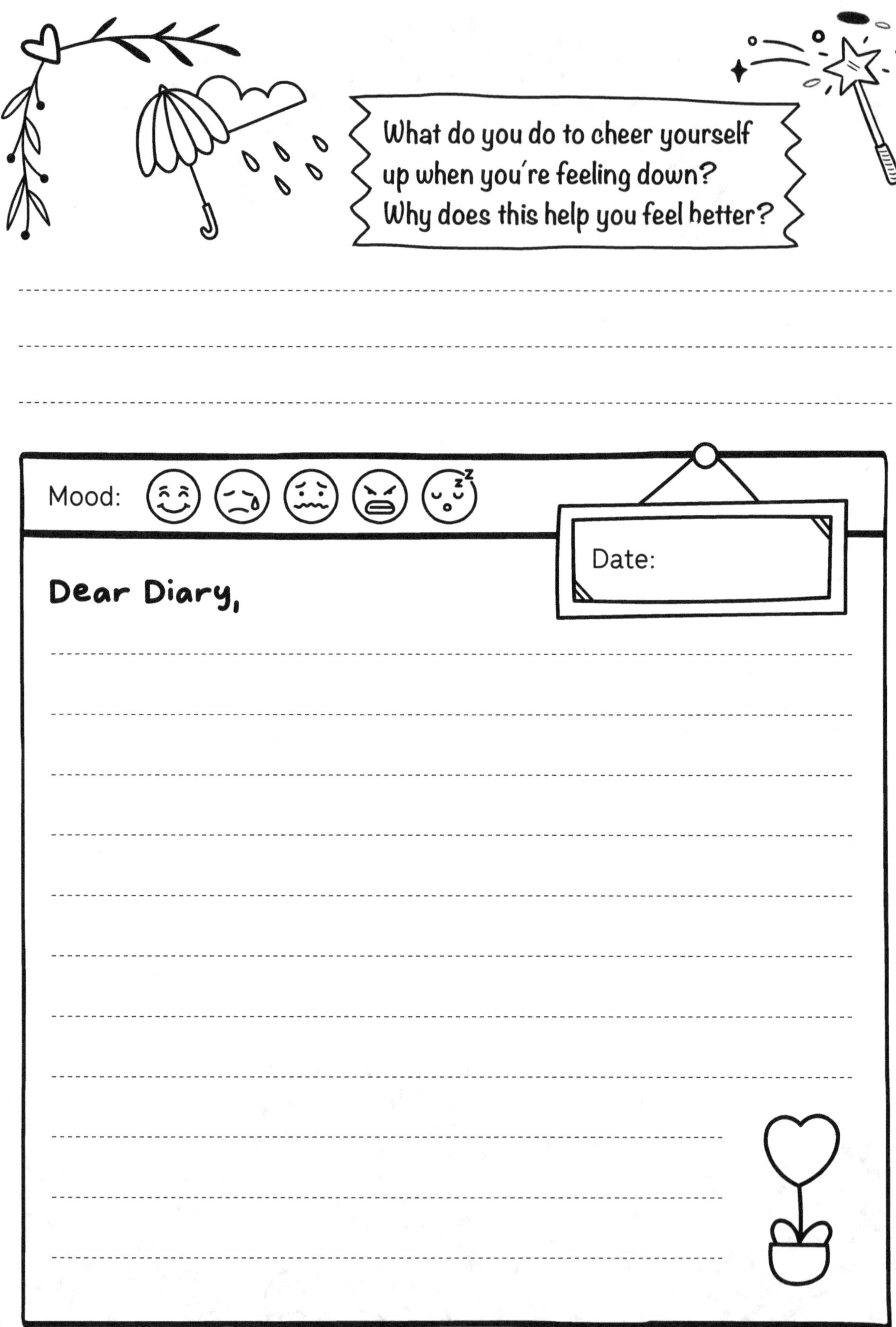

What do you do to cheer yourself up when you're feeling down? Why does this help you feel better?

Mood:

Date:

Dear Diary,

ACTIVITIES WITH FRIENDS AND FAMILY

"Alone we can do so little;
together we can do so much."

-Helen Keller

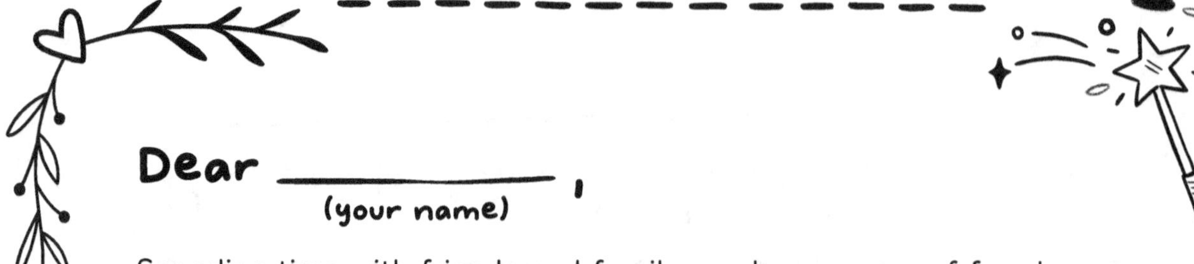

Dear ___________,
(your name)

Spending time with friends and family can be a source of fun, love, growth, and play. Sometimes it's challenging, since everyone has their own way of expressing love, and may enjoy different things than you do. But both friends and family can make your life brighter by showing you that there are different ways to be human, and each one of us has a unique presence in the world.

Playing games, going on adventures, or just spending time together are all ways that you can create memories with your friends and family. And all the time you spend together helps you build stronger bonds of love, trust, and communication.

Remember that being with friends and family can also teach you important life lessons like cooperation, communication, forgiveness, and empathy. When you learn to work together as a team, solve problems, and support each other through the good and bad times, it will also help you on your journey of growing up in the world.

Take a moment to reflect on all the beautiful times you've shared with friends and family, and how each person in your life is unique—just like you.

In this section, you will enjoy activities with friends and family.
We will build strong bonds through friendship, support,
teamwork, fun, memories, traditions, adventure, and laughter.

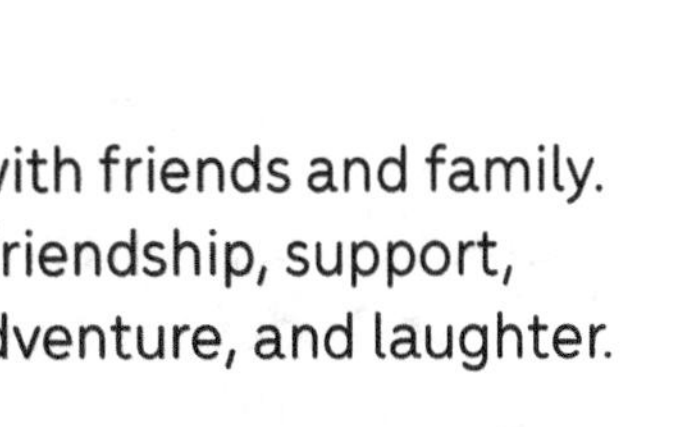

MEMORIES:

"I create lasting and cherished memories with friends and family."

SUPPORT:

"I am a source of support and encouragement for my loved ones."

TEAMWORK:

"I enjoy working together with others."

FRIENDSHIP:

"I build strong and lasting bonds with my friends."

FUN:

"I find joy and excitement in shared activities."

TRADITIONS:

"I value and enjoy making family traditions."

ADVENTURE:

"I explore and have adventures with those I love."

LAUGHTER:

"I share joy and happiness with friends and family."

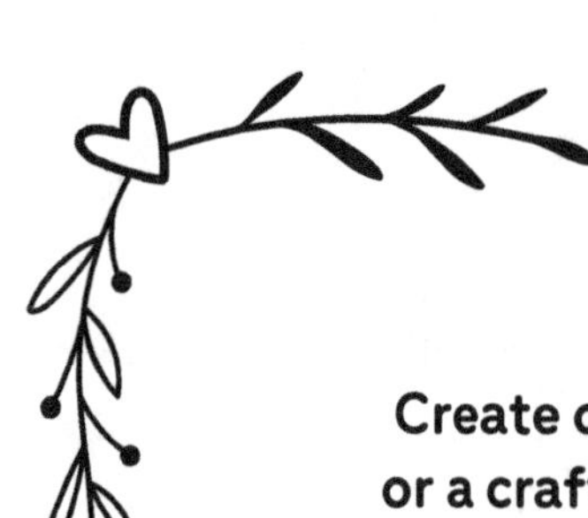

Experience Coupons

Create coupons for fun activities like a movie night, a picnic, or a craft day with your friends and family. Decorate each one, then distribute them to your friends and family as a surprise.

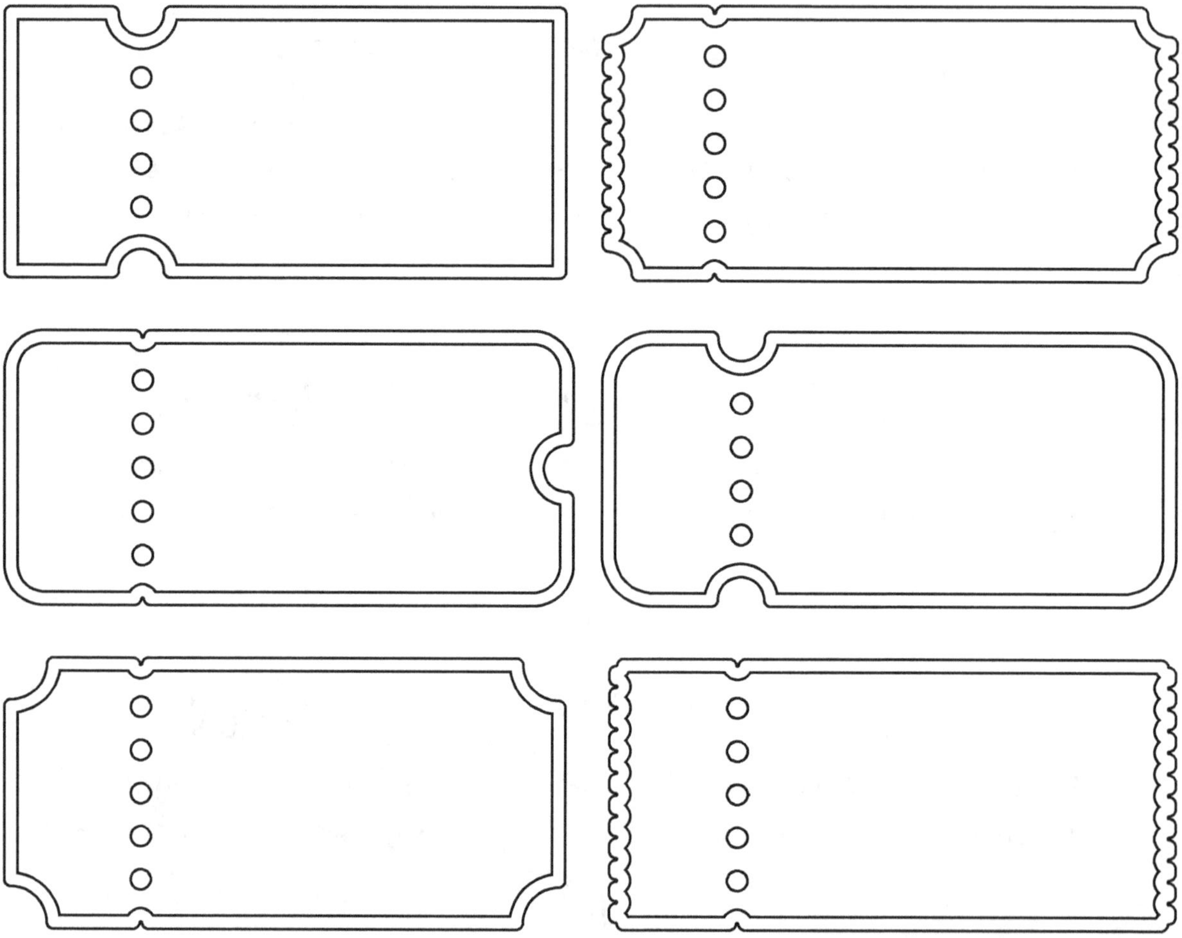

Describe a fun activity you did with a friend or family member recently. What made it special?

Mood:

Dear Diary,

Date:

Craft Corner: Friendship Bracelets and Cards

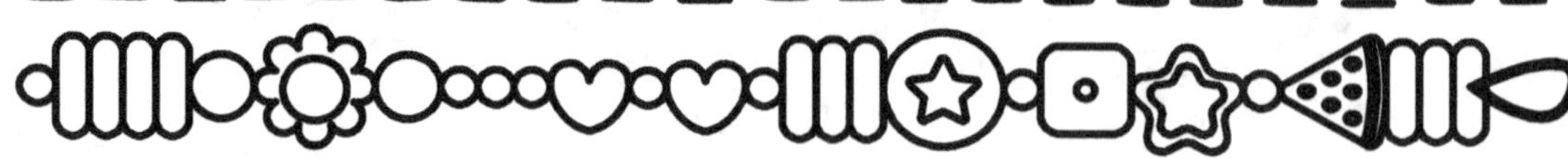

Follow these step-by-step guides to create something special for your loved ones.

♥ **Step #1:** Gather Materials: Collect beads, threads, cards, and any other decorative items you'd like to use for your bracelets or cards. Choose a variety of colors and textures to make your creations unique.

♥ **Step #2:** Choose Your Design: Decide on the design for your friendship bracelets or cards. You can find inspiration online or come up with your own creative ideas. Consider the preferences of the person you're making them for and what you think would best reflect them in your design.

♥ **Step #3:** Prepare Your Workspace: Set up a comfortable and well-lit workspace. Lay out your materials neatly so you can easily access them while crafting.

3 Tips for Crafting

- **Personalize:** Personalize each bracelet or card with the recipient's name, favorite colors, or symbols that hold special meaning to them.

- **Share Your Creations:** Give your friendship bracelets or cards to your loved ones as heartfelt gifts. Explain the significance of your designs and the effort you put into making them.

- **Enjoy:** Wear your friendship bracelets proudly or display your cards where you can see them. Cherish the memories of crafting something special for the people you care about.

If you are crafting friendship bracelets . . .

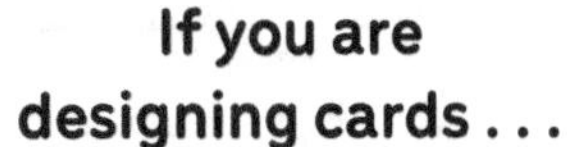

- Cut several strands of thread, each about 24 inches long, in different colors.
- Tie the strands together at one end, leaving a small loop.
- Secure the loop to a stationary object or safety pin it to your clothing to hold it in place.
- Begin braiding the strands together, alternating colors as desired.
- Continue braiding until the bracelet reaches the desired length, leaving a small tail at the end.
- Tie a knot at the end to secure the braid and trim any excess thread.

If you are designing cards . . .

- Fold your cardstock or paper in half to create a card.
- Use markers, colored pencils, or paint to decorate the front of the card with your chosen design.
- Add personal messages, drawings, or embellishments to make the card special.
- Write a heartfelt message inside the card to show your appreciation for the recipient.

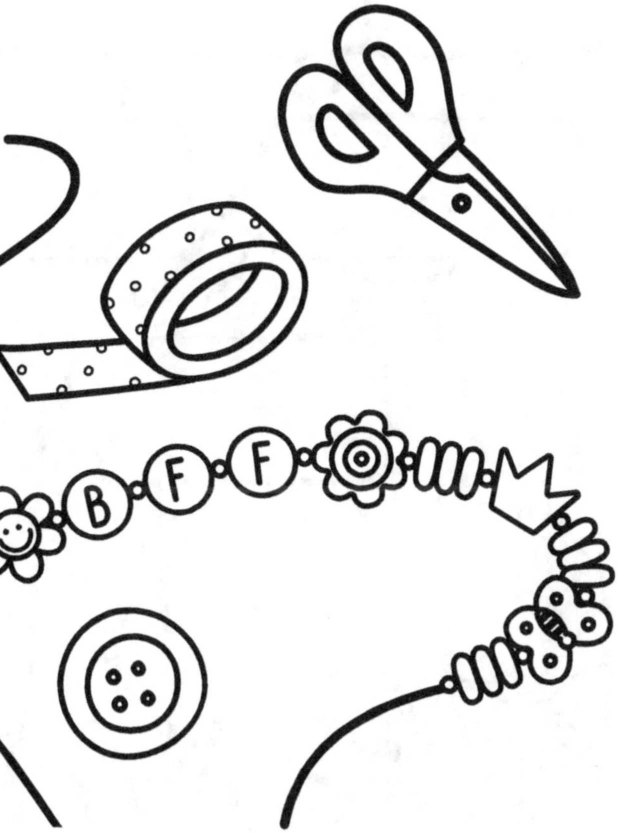

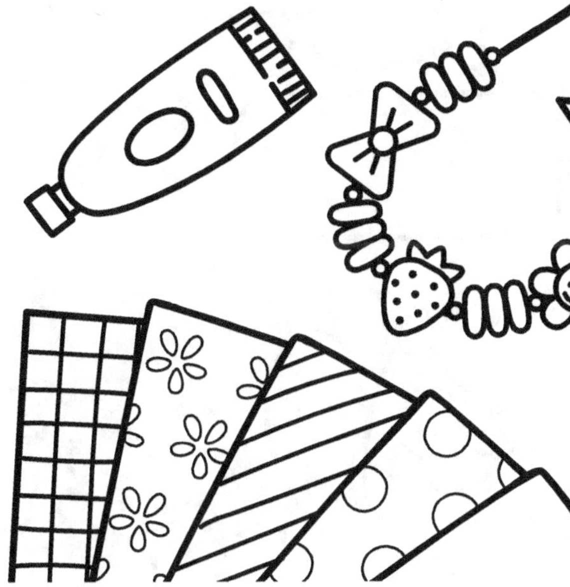

My Family Tree

Draw and describe your family members.
What makes each of them special to you?
Add fun facts or memories about each person.

What is your favorite family tradition and why? Describe how it makes you feel.

Mood:

Dear Diary,

Date:

"Surround yourself with only people who are going to lift you higher."
-Oprah Winfrey

Friendship Map

Draw your neighborhood or the places that are important to you and your friends. Plot your friendships and shared experiences on this map. Where did you meet? What do you love doing together? Draw little icons to represent different activities.

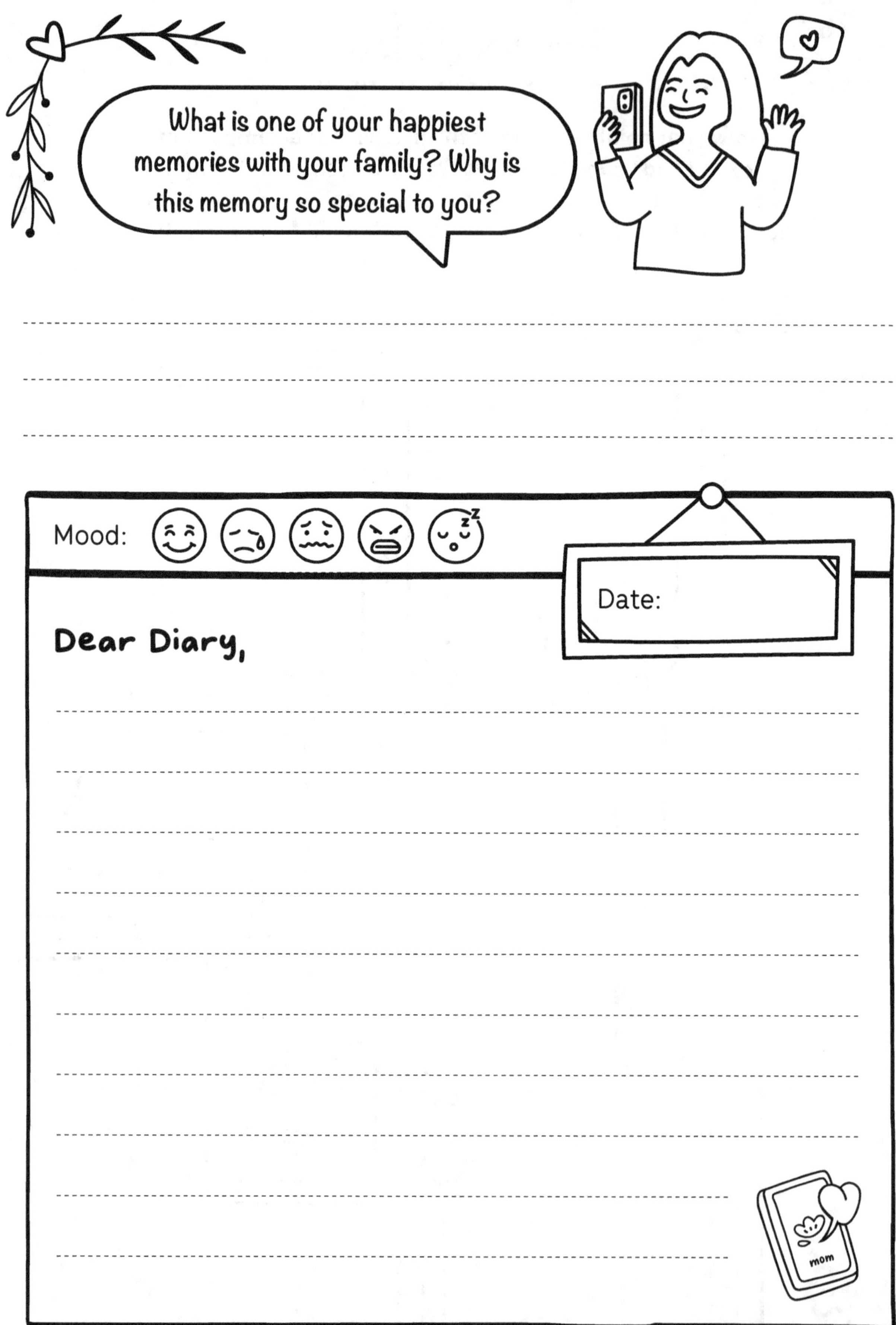

What is one of your happiest memories with your family? Why is this memory so special to you?

Mood:

Dear Diary,

Date:

mom

Letters to Friends and Family

Write a letter to a friend or family member telling them how much they mean to you. Share a favorite memory or a reason why you appreciate them.

My Gallery of Memories

Draw your favorite memories with friends and family.
Add captions to each drawing. You can also paste photos if you have them.

What qualities do you admire in your best friend? How does your best friend make you a better person?

Mood:

Date:

Dear Diary,

Acting with My Friends

Write a short play and act it out with your friends.
Let your imagination run wild! Create characters,
a plot, and dialogue that will bring your story to life.

Letters to Friends and Family

Write a letter to someone who has been kind to you recently.
How did their kindness impact you?

What is something new you want to try with your family? How do you think it will bring you closer?

Mood:

Date:

Dear Diary,

REFLECTIONS AND THE FUTURE

Dear ______________,
(your name)

As we get to the end of this journal, take a moment to slow down and reflect on the journey you've taken. Look back at how you discovered yourself, connected to your creativity, expressed your feelings, and found joy with friends and family.

Reflection is a special part of growing up. As you get older there will be more and more memories for you to look back on, like a piggy bank that's stored up for a rainy day. When you take a moment to reflect, it's like sitting in the mirror and looking at yourself. Some days you look different, and some reflections hold joy while others might hold different emotions.

But remember that all your reflections and memories can be used to help you throughout life. When you think of the big dreams you have for the future, maybe you draw on some of the life lessons you've learned in the past.

The world is full of endless possibilities, but you have to tap into your potential to find them. Slowing down each day and taking a moment to connect to your heart is a wonderful way to realize the potential you carry.

What are your passions? What are your goals? What are your dreams? When you take a moment to slow down and think about these questions, you can start to manifest them into being.

You have the ability to shape your future. Never forget that you carry the determination, strength, and courage to achieve anything you truly desire.

In this section, you will reflect on your past and plan for the future. We will focus on dreams, goals, learning, and growth, evolving over time to become the best version of ourselves and use our talents to help others.

HOPE:
"I believe in positive outcomes and have hope for the future."

RESILIENCE:
"I overcome challenges and grow stronger each day."

GOALS:
"I set and achieve my goals with determination."

DREAMS:
"I dream big and plan for an amazing future."

LEARNING:
"I gain wisdom from all my experiences."

ACHIEVEMENT:
"I celebrate my successes and achievements."

GROWTH:
"I am constantly growing and evolving."

VISION:
"I have a clear vision of my future self and my path."

Letter to My Future Self

Write a letter to your future self about your hopes, reminders, and expectations. What do you want to achieve? What do you want to remember?

What are you most excited about for the future?
Why does it excite you? What is something that worries
you about the future, but you trust you will overcome?

Mood:

Date:

Dear Diary,

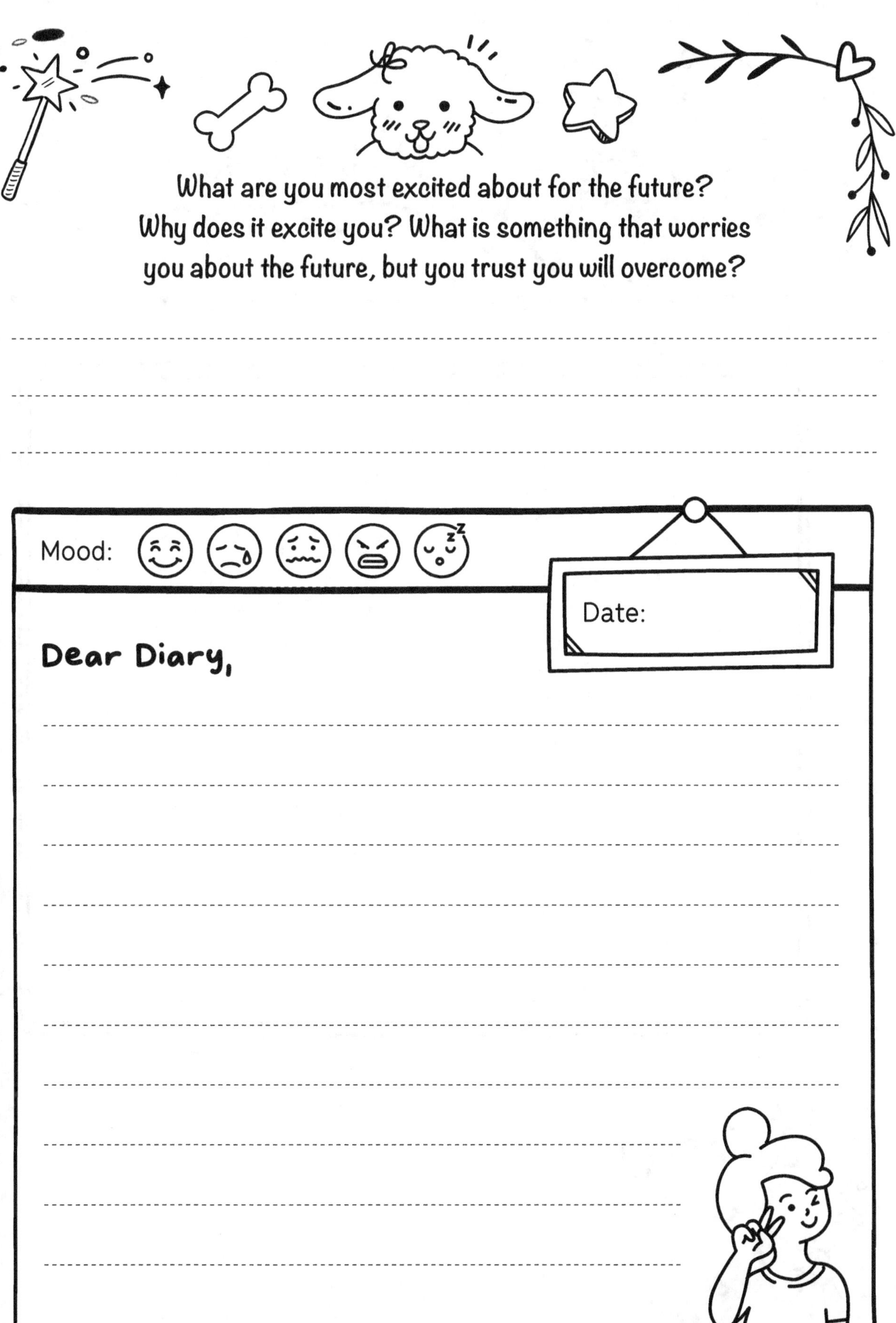

My Vision Board

What are your dreams? What do you want to achieve?
Where do you want to go? Use magazine cut-outs, drawings,
and words to make a vision board inside the pages of your journal.

My Biggest Dream

Illustrate your biggest dream. What does it look like?
How does it make you feel? Use bright colors to bring your dream to life.

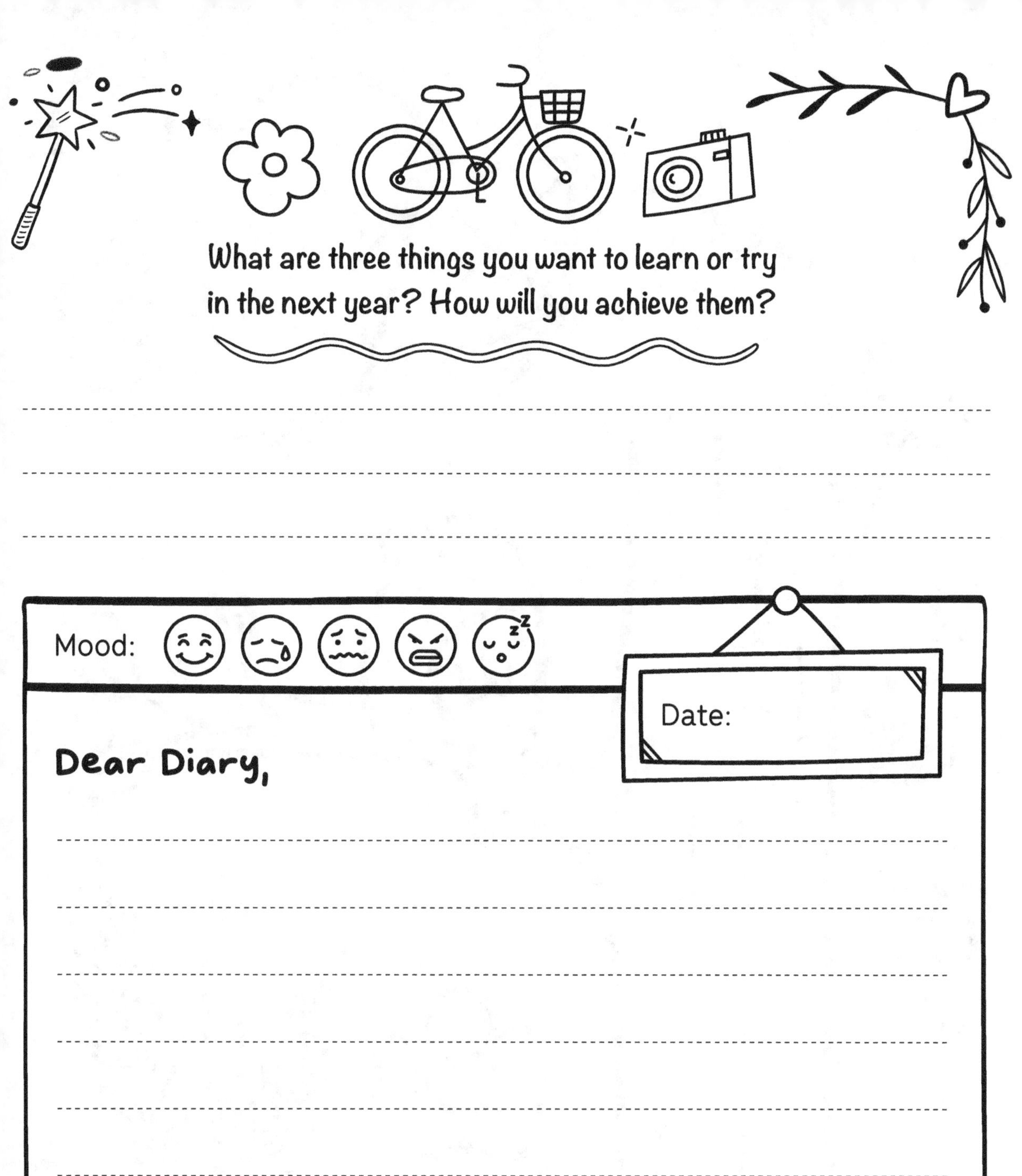

What are three things you want to learn or try in the next year? How will you achieve them?

Mood:

Date:

Dear Diary,

"The future belongs to those who believe in the beauty of their dreams."
-Eleanor Roosevelt

My Future Plans

Write down your goals. What steps will you take to achieve them? Write down the small steps that will help you reach your bigger dreams.

Start

Write about a person who inspires you.
What qualities do they have that you admire?
How do they motivate you to be your best self?
Mood:
Date:
Dear Diary,

My Habits Old and New

List the habits you want to start or stop doing.

What new habits do you want to start?

☆ --

☆ --

☆ --

☆ --

☆ --

☆ --

☆ --

What old habits do you want to let go of?

My Bucket List

List activities you want to experience in the future.

What adventures are
you excited about?

Why do they interest you?

What is a place you dream of visiting and why? Describe what you would do there and how it would feel.

Mood:

Date:

Dear Diary,

My Dream Home

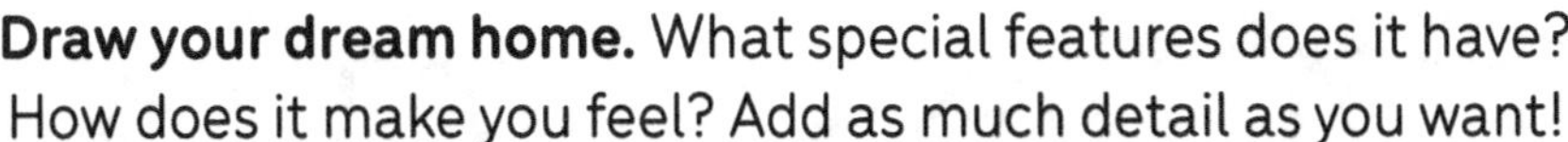

Draw your dream home. What special features does it have?
How does it make you feel? Add as much detail as you want!

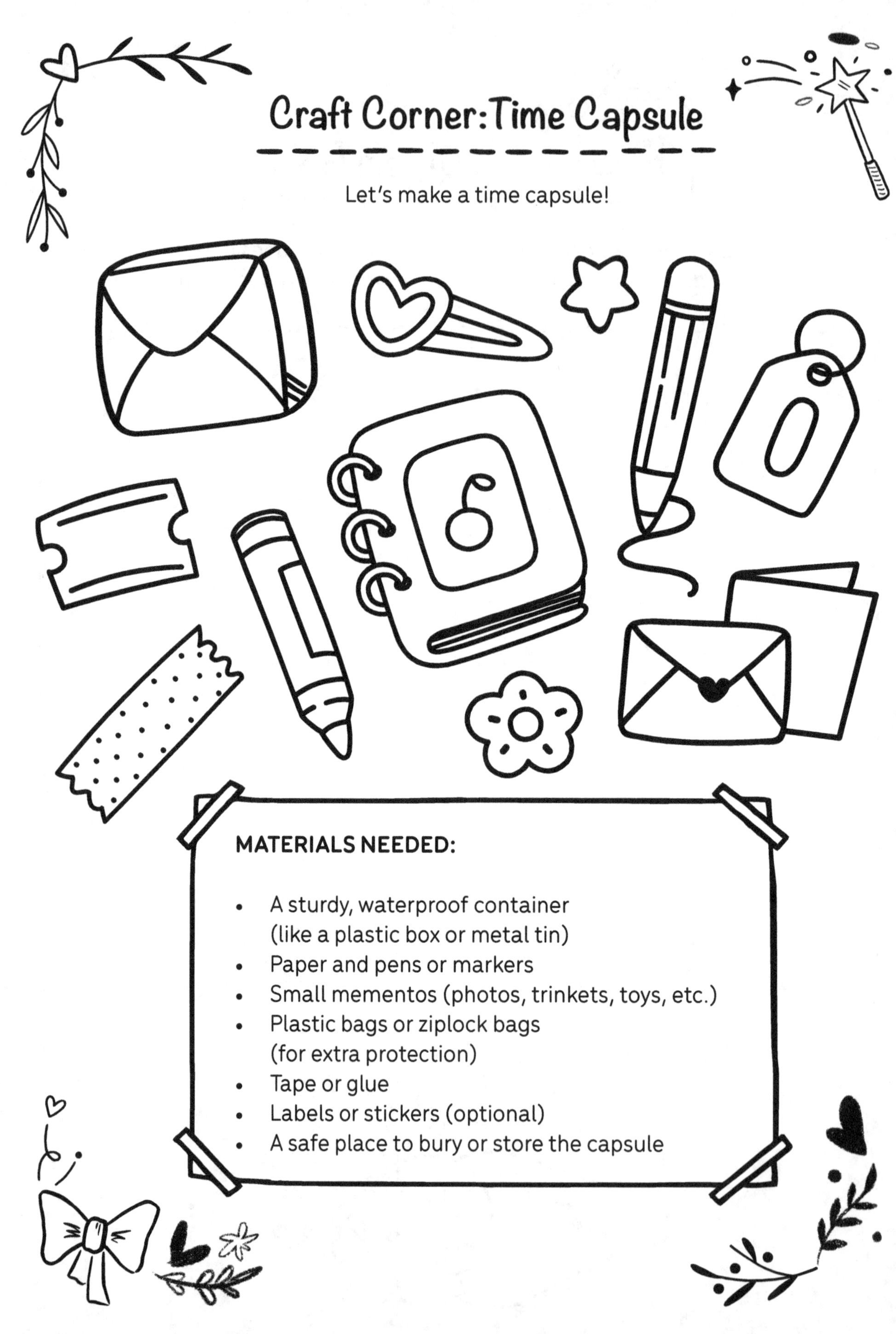

Craft Corner: Time Capsule

Let's make a time capsule!

MATERIALS NEEDED:

- A sturdy, waterproof container
  (like a plastic box or metal tin)
- Paper and pens or markers
- Small mementos (photos, trinkets, toys, etc.)
- Plastic bags or ziplock bags
  (for extra protection)
- Tape or glue
- Labels or stickers (optional)
- A safe place to bury or store the capsule

INSTRUCTIONS:

1. <u>Choose Your Container:</u>
   - Find a container that is waterproof and durable. This will protect your items from weather and time.

2. <u>Collect Your Treasures:</u>
   - Gather items that are special to you and represent your life right now. This could include:
     - ◊ A letter to your future self
     - ◊ Photos of friends and family
     - ◊ Small toys or trinkets
     - ◊ Drawings or crafts you've made
     - ◊ A list of your favorite things (books, movies, songs, etc.)
     - ◊ A newspaper or magazine from the current date

3. <u>Write Your Letter:</u>
   - Write a letter to your future self. Include your dreams, goals, favorite memories, and what life is like right now. You can also include predictions for the future!

4. <u>Protect Your Items:</u>
   - Place paper items in plastic bags to keep them dry. You can also wrap fragile items in tissue paper or bubble wrap.

5. <u>Decorate Your Container:</u>
   - Use stickers, labels, or markers to decorate your time capsule. Write your name and the date on the outside. You can also add a note like "Do not open until [date]!"

6. <u>Seal Your Capsule:</u>
   - Once everything is inside and protected, seal your container tightly. Use tape or glue to make sure it stays closed.

7. <u>Choose a Spot:</u>
   - Decide where you will store or bury your time capsule. It could be in your backyard, a garden, or even a special spot in your house. Make sure it's a place you'll remember and can access later.

8. <u>Mark the Date:</u>
   - Decide when you want to open your time capsule. Write this date down somewhere you won't forget, like a calendar or journal.

9. <u>Store or Bury:</u>
   - Place your time capsule in its spot. If you're burying it, dig a hole deep enough to cover the container completely. If you're storing it indoors, find a safe place where it won't be disturbed.

10 <u>Wait Patiently:</u>
   - Now, all you have to do is wait! It can be exciting to think about the future and what you'll discover when you finally open your time capsule.

ENJOY THE JOURNEY:

- Creating a time capsule is a wonderful way to capture the present and look forward to the future. When you open it, you'll have a special glimpse into your past and see how much you've grown and changed!

What message do you want to leave for your future self in the time capsule? What advice or words of encouragement would you give?

Mood:

Date:

Dear Diary,

What do you hope will be
different in your life five years
from now? What do you want
to stay the same?

"You cannot hope to build a better world without improving the individuals. To that end, each of us must work for our own improvement and, at the same time, share a general responsibility for all humanity."

-Marie Curie

Dear ___________ ,
(your name)

As you reach the end of this diary, I hope you feel proud of all the thoughts, dreams, and creations you've shared. This is just the beginning of your incredible journey. Continue to express yourself, cherish your memories, and dream big.

Always remember, you are loved and capable of achieving anything you set your mind to.

Sav Lucia is a passionate writer with over five years of experience in creating content that inspires emotional growth, creativity, and self-discovery. Her writing focuses on helping readers, especially children, explore their inner thoughts and emotions, offering them a safe space to express themselves.

Having been homeschooled, Sav's deep love of books and learning has always been at the heart of her work. She believes that journaling and quiet reflection can provide powerful tools for self-understanding and personal growth. Through her work, she aims to guide young readers in discovering their strengths, building confidence, and contributing positively to the world around them.

Sav holds a B.A. in Philosophy, Religion, and Anthropology from The New School in New York City, graduating with merit. She currently resides in the United Kingdom, where she continues to write and create meaningful content for young audiences.